Contents

Rocks in space

When the Sun and the planets were made, lots of pieces of rock were left over. Millions of these rocks fly around in space today.

WOW!

Sometimes rocks from space crash into planets and moons. The biggest rocks make holes where they land. These holes are called craters.

4

Big rocks that fly around, or orbit, the Sun are called asteroids (see below). Smaller rocks are meteoroids. Comets are giant balls of ice and rock. They are like huge rocky snowballs in space.

On a clear night you can sometimes see a comet from Earth.

The solar system

In the centre of our solar system is the Sun. The Sun is a star. It sends out the heat and light we call sunshine.

Eight planets travel around (or orbit) the Sun. Lots of space rocks also orbit the Sun.

Mar

Jupiter

There are millions of asteroids between Mars and Jupiter.

Mercury

Venus

Earth

Earth's Moon

The planets are Mercury, Venus, Earth, Mars, Jupiter, Saturn, Uranus and Neptune.

Dwarf planets also go around the Sun. Pluto is a dwarf planet. The Sun, the planets and other space objects make up the solar system.

Uranus

Neptune

Pluto (dwarf planet)

Saturn

What is a comet?

If you see a bright ball with a long
tail in the night sky, it may be a comet.
These lumps of rock and ice are like
huge snowballs flying around the Sun.

WOW!

Most comets
have two tails.
One is light blue
and made of gas.
The other is brighter
and made of dust.

If a comet flies close to the Sun, it begins to melt. A long tail forms behind it. The tail can be millions of kilometres long!

Halley's Comet

Some comets take thousands of years to orbit the Sun. Others take a lot less time. One called Halley's Comet takes about 75 years. We can see it from Earth. We last saw it in 1986. We may see the comet again in 2061.

WOW!
Comets look bright because the dust they give off shines in sunlight.

A spacecraft called *Giotto* took photos of Halley's Comet in 1986. The comet looks like a big, lumpy rock. Jets of gas and dust are flying out of it.

Giotto

Finding out about comets

Scientists wanted to know more about comets. In 2006, they sent a spacecraft called *Deep Impact* to visit one.

In 2006 a spacecraft called *Stardust* flew past a comet. It caught some of the comet's dust and sent it back to Earth.

When *Deep Impact* was close,
it sent out a metal missile. This made
a hole in the comet. A cloud of dust,
gas, rock and ice came flying out.

Deep Impact

13

What is an asteroid?

Asteroids are big pieces of rock and metal in space. Thousands of them race around the Sun. Most asteroids are in the asteroid belt between Mars and Jupiter.

This very big asteroid is called Vesta. It is 578 km wide. The surface is mainly a rock called lava.

Some asteroids are a few metres
across. Others are much bigger.
Asteroids can be different colours.
Shiny asteroids are mainly metal.

Finding out about asteroids

Asteroids are mostly a very long way away from Earth. Scientists sent a spacecraft to look at one called Eros. The craft flew around it, then landed on it. It sent photos back to Earth.

WOW!

Eros travels around the Sun at 87,000 kph. That's more than 10 times faster than a jet plane!

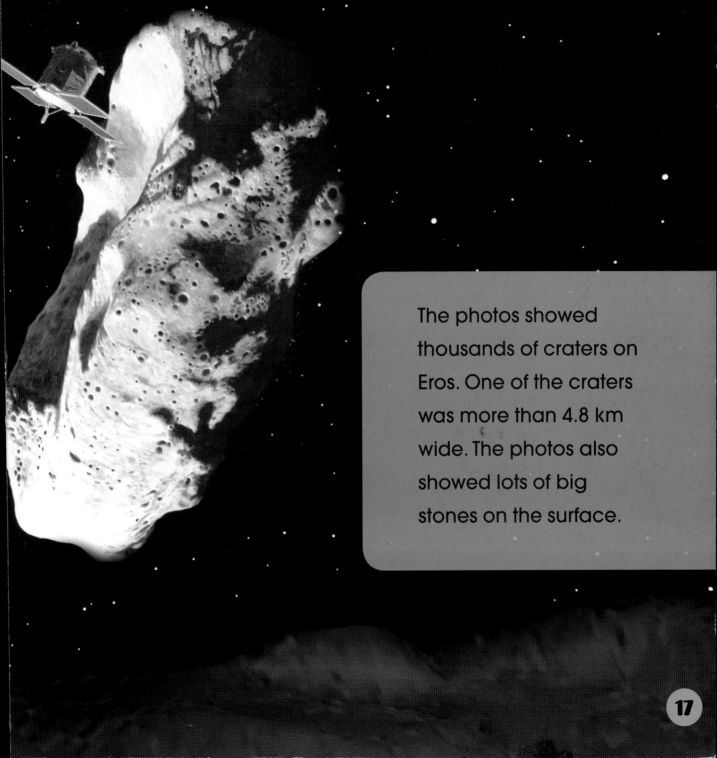

The photos showed thousands of craters on Eros. One of the craters was more than 4.8 km wide. The photos also showed lots of big stones on the surface.

Shooting stars

On a clear night you might see a streak of light in the sky – a shooting star. It is not really star, but a meteor.

Most shooting stars are tiny. Some are smaller than a grain of sand. We see them because they shine so brightly.

Meteors are small pieces of meteoroid rock. They fly into the atmosphere. This is the air around Earth. The rock gets so hot that it burns up and changes to gas. Then we see it as a streak of light.

Meteorites

Many small space rocks burn up in the air. Bigger rocks can fall to the ground. Then they are called meteorites.

Meteorites are made of stone or metal, or a mixture of both.

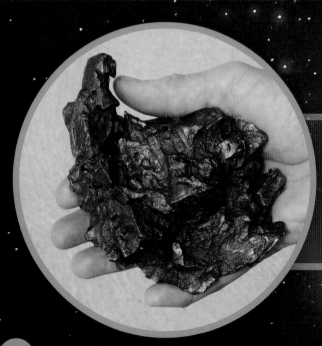

Many meteorites are small. They would fit in an adult's hand.

Big meteorites have fallen to Earth, and some have made huge craters. The meteorite that made this one in Arizona hit Earth at about 42,000 kph. The crater is more than 1,220 m wide and 150 m deep.

Make a comet

What you need

Pieces of foil

Lengths of ribbon (one colour or different colours)

What to do

1. Take a piece of foil and crumple it into the shape of a bow.

2. Tie some pieces of ribbon around the middle of the bow. Leave long ends for the tail of the comet.

3. Crumple both sides of the foil around the ribbon to hold it in place. The ribbon should poke out of one end.

4. Wrap more pieces of foil around the comet to make it bigger.

5. Throw your comet to make it fly! See if your comet flies further than your friends' comets.

Useful words

asteroid
A big rock that orbits the Sun.
An asteroid can be just a
few metres across or
hundreds of kilometres wide.

atmosphere
The layer of gases around
a planet, moon or star.

comet
A ball of rock, dust and ice
that orbits the Sun.

meteor
The streak of light made by
a piece of space rock that
burns as it travels through
the Earth's atmosphere.
Also called a shooting star.

meteorite
A piece of space rock
that lands on Earth.

meteoroid
A piece of space rock from
a comet or asteroid that
orbits the Sun.

orbit
To move around another
object.

planet
A large object in space that
orbits the Sun or another star.

Find out more

Websites

www.esa.int/esaKIDSen/
Cometsandmeteors.html

www.kidsastronomy.com/asteroid.
htm

www.kidscosmos.org/solar_
system/asteroids_comets_meteors.
php

Books

Asteroids and Comets
(Space), Ian Graham
(Franklin Watts, 2016)

First Fabulous Facts Space,
Anita Ganeri (Ladybird, 2014)

Index